Elizabethan Madrigal Dinners

Elizabethan Madrigal Dinners

Scripts, with Music for Singers, Players, and Dancers

JOHN HABERLEN

and

STEPHEN ROSOLACK

INSTRUMENTAL PARTS FOR SALE BY THE PUBLISHER

Set I Instrumental parts for Part I of Elizabethan Madrigal Dinners
Set II Instrumental parts for Part II of Elizabethan Madrigal Dinners
Set III Instrumental parts for Part III of Elizabethan Madrigal Dinners

Published by

Mark Foster

MUSIC COMPANY

Box 4012, Champaign, IL 61820

Library of Congress Card Number 78-70082

Paperback Edition ISBN 0-916656-09-8

Wire Bound Edition ISBN 0-916656-12-8

Printed in the United States of America

Typeset by Francisco's TypoGraphics

Music by Mark Foster Music Company

Current Printing (last digit)

10 9 8 7 6 5 4 3 2

PREFACE

Increasingly, school and church groups are celebrating the Yuletide with festive dinners. Madrigals, carols, dances, ceremony, and dialogue lead to exciting dramatic productions. These celebrations in the milieu of some specific historical period, such as the Renaissance, are especially rewarding experiences for both performers and audience.

Inherent in such productions is the difficulty of constructing a program with appropriate music and dialogue, especially if one seeks some degree of authenticity.

Elizabethan Madrigal Dinners helps solve these time-consuming problems by providing ready-to-use material: scripts of two dinners with performance editions of the Renaissance music. The regular paperback edition is for libraries and reference, while the wirebound edition is for singers, accompanists, and the conductor. Instrumental parts are available in three supplemental packets, each including parts for C, Bb, F, and alto-clef instruments.

Set I contains the instrumental parts for the music in Part I, Music for Singers with Players.

Set II is for Part II, Music for Dancers and Players, and,

Set III is for Part III, Music of familiar carols for Singers, Players, and Audience, for use as background music during the dinner and for audience participation.

The music and scripts found in *Elizabethan Madrigal Dinners* provide a wealth of material for the creation of a memorable event.

ACKNOWLEDGEMENTS

The authors are grateful to those who have contributed to *Elizabethan Madrigal Dinners; Scripts, with Music for Singers, Players, and Dancers.* Our thanks go to Charles Knox for his arrangements of *The Holly and The Ivy* and *Wassail Carol*, and his keyboard realization of *Sweet Was the Song*; to Margita Haberlen for her English translation of *Josef, Lieber Josef Mein* and *Allon, Gay Bergeres*; to Michael Anderson for his keyboard reduction of *A Christmas Carol*; to David Lewman for the additional stanzas to *Flaming Pudding*; to Dennis Martin, for his edition of *Angelus ad Virginem*, and to Dr. James McKelvy for his careful and creative suggestions about the content and format of the text and music.

We especially appreciate the enthusiasm and suggestions from the participants in our Madrigal Dinners at the University of Illinois, Urbana-Champaign.

J.H. & S.R.

INTRODUCTION

Elizabethan Madrigal Dinners contains all the music and dialogue necessary for the production of a madrigal dinner in the style of the late 16th century. This period was the height of the Renaissance during which England was ruled by Queen Elizabeth (1558–1603). All the selections in this collection, with the exception of the *Wassail Carol, The Holly and the Ivy,* and the traditional Christmas carols, were composed before or during her reign.

The order of the dinner's festive events:

I. Arrival and Seating of Guests

II. Pre-Dinner Ceremony

- A. Procession
- B. Greetings to Guests

III. Dinner Ceremony

- A. The Wassail Bowl
- B. Toasting
- C. The Boar's Head
- D. Serving the Dinner
- E. The Flaming Pudding
- F. Table Serenades by Strolling Carolers

IV. After-Dinner Pageant

- A. Dialogue
- B. Songs
- C. Dances
- D. Recessional

Elizabethan Madrigal Dinners includes two scripts for the pageant. They are similar in style, but different in content and choice of music. Directors may wish to adapt the dialogue to different audiences, and to substitute other music to fit the performance capabilities of the singers and dancers. To retain the Renaissance flavor, these alternate compositions should be of the 16th Century. While familiar Christmas carols usually postdate the Renaissance, this music fits well into such a seasonal occasion.

The dinner tables should be decorated in a festive manner and placed around the stage area, which is the focal point in the hall. Decorated with banners and pennants, and adorned with wreaths and garlands of holly and ivy, the hall will exude a holiday atmosphere.

The use of subtle stage lighting creates a close rapport between the performers and audience. Dimmers will help to keep this in balance, as will candles, if local fire ordinances permit.

Dress the singers, dancers, and instrumentalists in Elizabethan costumes. These can be rented for the occasion, although at some expense. Students may be able to design and sew their own costumes.

Some props are essential: a large wassail bowl with cups for each performer, and a paper-mache boar's head. The boar's head is brought into the hall on a huge platter decked with fruits and greens. Some productions may wish to use a real cooked pig's head with a fresh apple in its mouth. At the entrance of the dessert, one might use a large flaming pudding for the performers' table, with individual cakes for the guests' tables.

The singers should deliver their lines with dramatic flair and a touch of a British accent. All the elements of good character acting need to be stressed by each person. The dialogue is best kept to a minimum, in order to allow a maximum of time for songs and dances. The entertainment may be varied by the additional humor and energy of magicians, jugglers, tumblers and court jesters.

The madrigal dinner is an excellent way to bring communities together to greet a holiday season.

TABLE OF CONTENTS

SCRIPTS

These scripts have been used successfully many times, and directors are encouraged to modify or extend the spoken parts to individualize the event. This freedom helped evolve the genre from a traditional after-dinner concert of madrigals to occasions which featured historical personalities such as King Henry VIII and Queen Elizabeth I. The freedom of alteration has sufficiently encouraged some directors to produce such diverse events as a dinner in the home of Benjamin Franklin and a Gay Nineties dinner with Queen Victoria and Prince Albert as hosts.

Good performance requires all of the acting abilities expected in a dramatic production. Speeches should be deliberate, and body movements exaggerated to assist the characterization of the personalities. Such attention to details will help create the atmosphere of a 16th century dinner.

AN ELIZABETHAN CHRISTMAS MADRIGAL DINNER

Script by John Haberlen

Originally Presented at the University of Illinois

John Haberlen, Director

THE CAST

The Singers portray members of Queen Elizabeth's Court, Sir William Byrd, Sir Francis Drake, Sir Walter Raleigh. A steward to carry in the boar's head and sing the carol is a necessity. Those who portray Elizabeth I and her consort need not be singers, but should be skilled dancers, so they can lead a dance. The dances may be performed by members of the singing ensemble, or by dancers. The instrumentalists, in costume, should be seated near the stage before the guests are admitted into the Hall.

THE PROGRAM

ARRIVAL OF GUESTS

Traditional and familiar Christmas carols are performed in the foyer or outer room of the dining hall as the dinner guests arrive.

SEATING THE GUESTS

When all are assembled, the Hall doors are opened and the guests are invited to be seated, as the instrumental consort plays Renaissance music.

PRE-DINNER CEREMONY

MUSIC: **Fanfare** (see page 70)
A lord and lady enter the Hall and present the following poem with clear ringing voices and a touch of British accent:

FIRST LORD.
 Let no man come into this hall,
 Groom, page nor yet marshall,
 But that some sport he bring withal
 For now is the time of Christmas.
FIRST LADY.
 If that he say he cannot sing,
 Some other sport then let him bring,

That it may please at this feasting,
For now is the time of Christmas.

FIRST LORD.

If that he say he can naught do,
Than for my love ask him no mo
But to the stocks then let him go,
For now is the time of Christmas.

Let us fill our Hall with greens and holly, for Gloriana, our Queen, will soon be in our presence.

PROCESSION OF THE GREENS

MUSIC: **Nowell Sing We** (see page 16)

All singers, in couples, enter with Nowell Sing We, *and process through the Hall, carrying strings of holly and ivy greens. They wind through the Hall, working their way to the stage where they add their holly and ivy to the decorations already on the stage.*

MUSIC: **The Holly and the Ivy** (see page 18)
Green Groweth the Ivy (see page 20)

DINNER CEREMONY

QUEEN *and her consort enter to a lively instrumental piece as the singers respond with bows and sotto voce* "Glorianna," "Good Queen Bess," etc. *Singers follow Queen and consort to their places at the table and seat themselves after the Queen has taken her place. Immediately there follows the sound of the head waiter at the door shouting* "Wassail" *three times. He enters the Hall quickly bringing the bowl to the main table on stage. Ad lib comments from the singers may be encouraged while the cups are being filled and passed to the cast. During this time, the audience is also being served. When everyone has cup in hand, the* SECOND LORD *speaks.*

SECOND LORD

Take your cups; Honor to you who sit,
near to the well of wit,
and drink your fill of it!

Audience and performers drink; performers may converse.

THIRD LORD *interrupting.*

A toast to our noble steeds!

LORDS *and* LADIES *all sing verse one of the* Wassail Song, *a quartet sings verse two, with voices and instruments joining in the chorus.*

FOURTH LORD.

A toast to our cows!

LORDS *and* LADIES *sing verse three with instruments, verse four* a cappella *and verse eight with instruments. During final chorus, singers pair off and leave the Hall. The instruments continue to play until all have exited, except the* FIFTH LORD.

MUSIC: **Fanfare, or three** forte **drum rolls** (see page 70)

FIFTH LORD:

It is said that long ago, a young student was studying in the quiet of Shotover Forest, when suddenly that quiet was broken, and he lowered his book of Aristotle to see charging him at full tilt a mighty, wild boar. Whereat the student raised his Aristotle again, but this time to ram it sharply into the boar's jaws with the cry: *Graecum est!* Thus, as the saying goes, *He choked the savage with the sage.* He brought the head back to be able to retrieve his good copy of Aristotle, and ever since, a boar's head has been borne to the table accompanied by the famous song: *The Boar's Head Carol.*

MUSIC: **Fanfare** (see page 70)

PROCESSION OF THE BOAR'S HEAD

The baritone designated to sing the Carol *enters, carrying the boar's head on a platter, holding it high. The singers, in couples, follow singing:*

MUSIC: **The Boar's Head Carol** (see page 23)

Immediately after the Processional, the guests are invited to begin the meal. Instrumentalists and singers may alternate in providing background dinner music. The instrumental ensemble may use material from Part II of this book, supplemented by other authentic Renaissance music. The singers may wish to divide into small ensembles to serenade from different parts of the Hall. When not singing, they should pass from table to table, greeting all, and creating a pleasant, festive mood. Before dessert is served, they should regroup for:

THE FLAMING PUDDING PROCESSIONAL

House lights dim.

MUSIC: **Flaming Pudding** (see page 25)

Instruments play, while the players, singing, line up on both sides of the entrance, leading the way to the stage. Waiters follow the singers then pass through them, carrying flaming puddings for each table of guests.

AFTER-DINNER ENTERTAINMENT

MUSIC: **Fanfare or three drum rolls** (see page 70)

FIRST LORD *alone on stage.*

Lords and Ladies, and Royal Guests: we trust thee hath feasted well. Now let merriment and mirth take place in the presence and countenance of Her Majesty, Queen Elizabeth, and Her Royal Court.

MUSIC: **Fanfare** (see page 70)
Instrumental Processional (see page 74)

QUEEN ELIZABETH *and* HER CONSORT *lead the procession of Lords and Ladies of the Court to her throne. The* QUEEN, *upon her arrival, turns and speaks:*

QUEEN ELIZABETH.
I bid thee welcome, to the great hall of Windsor Castle.

COURT.
God Save the Queen!

QUEEN.
I thank you, mine good people. Let the Christmas festivities commence.

SECOND LADY.
Thy servant, William Byrd (BYRD *steps forward and bows to the* QUEEN), of the Royal Chapel, has composed in thine honor "A Carol for Christmas Day."

MUSIC: **An Earthly Tree a Heavenly Fruit** (see page 28)
Two sopranos perform the song, accompanied by a harpsichord and/or four instruments.

MUSIC: **Cast Off All Doubtful Care** (see page 31)

QUEEN.
"As the heart ruleth over all the members, so music overcomes the heart." I thank thee, Sir William Byrd. (QUEEN *acknowledges the musicians, who bow in return.*) Good singers all, do please now sing that touching medieval carol, *Angelus ad Virginem,* written by our illustrious forebearer, Geoffrey Chaucer.

MUSIC: **Angelus ad Virginem** (see page 57)

THIRD LADY.
We wish to offer Your Majesty a most famous *chanson* composed by the well-known French musician, Guillame Costeley.

MUSIC: **Allon, Gay, Gay Bergeres** (see page 36)

QUEEN.

Sir Francis Drake, what have ye pirated from Spanish soil?

DRAKE.

Your Majesty, for what the dog-hearted Spaniards lacked with their Armada, the musicians have proved to be of considerable merit as with this vigorous carol.

MUSIC: **Riu, Riu, Chiu** (Associated Music Co.)

QUEEN.

'Tis not *too* vulgar for a Spanish carol. What new have ye from the Rhineland?

FOURTH LADY.

Your Majesty, a lovely lullaby which contains a melody of substantial grace.

MUSIC: **Josef, lieber Josef mein** (see page 43)

QUEEN.

Quite lovely. Sir Walter Raleigh, it is nice that ye are among us this Christmas. Have ye a wish of the Court?

RALEIGH *bowing low.*

Good Queen Elizabeth, what would a feast be without a Branle, which doth quicken both our limbs and our spirits!

QUEEN.

Ye have my allowance. Royal Musicians! The official Branle!

MUSIC: **The Official Branle** (see page 79)

QUEEN.

Such good success pleases me.

RALEIGH.

And *I*, only . . . would that Your Gracious Majesty favor her Court and lead us in a dance!

COURT *with ad lib remarks of encouragement.*

QUEEN

So be it. Royal Musicians, I command thee to present the Court a grand Pavanne of commendable grace! Follow it with a Galliard of lively agility!

MUSIC: **Pavanne** (see page 74)
Galliard (see page 76)

When the QUEEN *solos on a chorus of the Galliard, the* COURT *comments, e.g.,* "She's wonderful!" "Such grace!"

QUEEN.

After such a strained feat, an air is in order which is designed to soothe and comfort my soul with the warmth of the season.

MUSIC: **Sweet Was The Song** (see page 50)
Soprano solo accompanied by harpsichord and/or four instruments.

QUEEN.
In truth, such beautiful music and dancing doth kindle the hearts of all good men. I thank thee one and all for such a display of these talents. Please, good sir: The Royal Proclamation!

FIRST LORD
Her Royal and Exalted Highness, Queen Elizabeth, wishes that the spirit of the holiday be with each of ye, and that the sights and sounds of this night fill the joys and peace of this season!

QUEEN.
Fare thee well, mine good people. I must be gone!

Singers group in couples to follow the QUEEN *out of the Hall while singing:*

MUSIC: **Recessional Carol: Joy to the World** (see page 101)

Singers retain the recessional order of two lines through which the guests pass as they leave the Hall, with the singers bidding each a farewell with season's greetings.

A LATE 16th CENTURY ENGLISH CHRISTMAS DINNER

Script by Stephen J. Rosolack

Originally Presented at the University of Illinois

Stephen J. Rosolack, Director

THE CAST

The singers;
LORD PHILLIP and LADY BARBARA of NOTTINGHAM
(HOSTS of the Dinner)
LORD and LADY CUMBERLAND
LORD and LADY WESTMORLAND
LORD and LADY WORCHESTER
LORD and LADY BERKSHIRE
LORD and LADY SOMERSET
LORD and LADY HINTINGDON
LORD and LADY CHESHIRE
LORD and LADY GLOUCESTER
STEWARD

The instrumentalists: In costume, they sit across the hall from the head tables. The director, also in costume, sits with them, to do any necessary cuing for both singers and instrumentalists.

THE PROGRAM

ARRIVAL AND SEATING OF GUESTS

Outside the hall, one half hour before the performance, traditional carols are sung as the guests arrive. About 15 minutes before curtain time, the doors may be opened for seating to begin. At this time, it is appropriate to have the instrumental ensemble inside the hall playing incidental music.

PRE-DINNER CEREMONY

At curtain time, the STEWARD and four assistants process into the hall and set the main tables with great ceremony. Ordinary wooden planks and horses may be used for the tables. They can then be removed after the meal to provide any additional space necessary for performance.

The lords and ladies in couples enter singing. They take their seats at the head table.

MUSIC: **Nowell, Sing We** (see page 16)
or, **Make We Joy Now In This Fest** (Musica Brittanica)

LORD PHILLIP.

Lords, Ladies, and Noble Guests! Lady Barbara and I bid you welcome to this hall, which, by our command, has been fitted for an evening of feasting, singing, and DANCING *(his passion)* for the general merriment of you all. May our evening of festivity recall the blessed event of Christmas which joins us all as men of good will. As has been our custom, Lady Barbara and I have annually invited guests from the reaches of our land to come and spend several days with us. Steward, present our guests.

STEWARD *reads the above list of guests. As each couple is introduced, they rise. The lord bows, and the lady curtsies to the other lords and ladies, and to the patrons in the hall. Applause will usually be generously extended to each couple. When that task is completed:*

So that good order and propriety may be maintained on this eve, I have been commanded by my Lord to remind you of the Rules of Etiquette which are observed by all at this court on such festive occasions. *(He produces a scroll with the rules upon it and reads:)*

Guests must have clean nails or they will disgust their table companions.

Guests must avoid quarreling and making grimaces with other guests.

Guests must not stuff their mouths. The glutton who eats with haste, if he is addressed, he rarely answers thee.

Guests should not pick their teeth at the table with a knife, straw or stick.

Guests must not tell unseemly tales at the table, not soil the cloth with their knife, nor rest their legs upon the table.

Guests must never leave bones on the table; always hide them under the chairs.

Guests must not wipe their greasy fingers on their beards.

Guests must not lean on the table with their elbows, nor dip their thumbs in their drink.

Guests must retain their knives or they shall be forced to grub with their fingers.

DINNER CEREMONY

LORD PHILLIP.

Steward! Let us have the Wassial bowl, so that we may wet out lips, warm our hearts, and offer our toasts!

The Wassail is served.

MUSIC: **Wassail Song** (see page 21)

The LORDS *then stand for toasting.*

LORD 1.

A toast to our Queen! To Elizabeth, the glory of our land. May health and happiness attend her. May every joy of the season be hers, and may she be blessed by Providence with longevity. To our Bess!

ALL.

To our Bess!

LORD 2.

A toast to the ladies in this hall! To them, who are the quiet strength of our lives, the rarest flowers of our courts, and the highest inspiration of our hearts! A toast to you all, our beloved ladies!

LORD 3.

And surely a toast to you, our gracious hosts! Lord Phillip and Lady Barbara of Nottingham! To our continued friendship, loyalty, and affection. To your hospitality in providing this splendid time of feasting and merriment. To your happiness and long life! To the Lord and Lady of Nottingham!

LORD PHILLIP.

We thank you, my dear friends, for your kind wishes and touching affection. NOW, let the feasting begin, for we have smelled the wondrous aromas the whole day long, and have grown ravenously hungry. My good Steward—we await you!

The instrumentalists play throughout the dinner, centrally or in two groups wandering about the hall.
All forms of spontaneous humor take place at the head table as the lords and ladies dine with the patrons. During the meal, the boar's head is brought in without previous announcement other than the beginning of the song.

MUSIC: **The Boar's Head Carol** (see page 23)

At the end of the meal, the flaming pudding is brought in and served. The pudding song accompanies the entrance of the delicacy.

MUSIC: **Flaming Pudding Carol** (see page 25)

AFTER-DINNER ENTERTAINMENT (PAGEANT)

LORD PHILLIP.

Lords and Ladies! Now, having partaken of such pleasing delicacies, and having restored our bodies, let us rise and amuse ourselves with some DANCING!

LADY BARBARA.

MY LORD! I beg you NAY! We have not yet visited with our guests in this hall—and perhaps dancing would be better undertaken after this meal has been allowed to settle and the tables have been cleared and removed from the hall.

LORD PHILLIP.

My dear Lady Barbara—as always I am well-advised. My friends, let us arise and stroll about the hall and visit with our guests.

The lords and ladies visit with the patrons, maintaining character in both bearing and in conversation. The STEWARD *and his assistants clear the main tables, and remove them from the hall. After all has been cleared, the singers organize themselves into two choirs on either side of the hall.*

LORD PHILLIP.

My good friends, one and all—let us sing together a carol in celebration. Good players, kindly set the pace for us!

MUSIC: **O Come All Ye Faithful** (see page 103)

All in the hall are invited to sing.

LORD 4 *to Lord Phillip.*

My Lord! May we favor this hall with a favorite tune called "Shepherds Rejoice" by our noble Thomas Morley?

LORD 5 *across the hall to Lord Phillip.*

My Lord! We should also hope to grace this hall with a little ditty composed by our Queen's father—Henry!

LORD PHILLIP.

Good people, let us by all means hear the tunes, and then let us hear another from everyone in the hall. My Lady and I will join this company in the Morley tune, for we know it well.

MUSIC: **Shepherds, Rejoice** (see page 62)
Pastime With Good Company (see page 54)
Deck the Halls (see page 88)

All in the hall are invited to sing.

LADY BARBARA.

My Lord! Such fine singing should not be put away so quickly. I pray you, request the singing books that we may enjoy some favorites not so easily remembered by the heart.

LORD PHILLIP.

Steward! Bring forth the singing books of this house and those which our friends brought with them.

Singers gather centrally in the hall. The part-books are passed out by the STEWARD. *One slight mix-up occurs:*

LADY 1.

Good Steward! I cannot sing a bass part!

LORD 6 *quickly.*

Nor I the soprano!

Copies are traded. Ad lib conversation takes place among the lords and ladies in deciding which of the pieces to sing. The sequence is as follows:

MUSIC: **Lo, How a Rose** (see page 56)
Angelus ad Virginem (see page 57)
Riu, Riu, Chiu (Associated Music Co.)

LORD PHILLIP.

Such music does truly charm the soul, but, my good company, let us NOW test our limbs and DANCE! My fine players, what have you assembled for us this evening?

DIRECTOR

My Lord, we have chosen a stately Pavanne, a spirited Galliard, AND, knowing my Lord's enthusiasm for the dance, we have chosen not just one Branle, but FOUR, so that this company may demonstrate its prowess and powers of variation.

LORD PHILLIP.

My good man, you shall be rewarded! My Lords and Ladies, let us take our places!

A lengthy and exciting dance segment takes place including the following:

MUSIC: **Pavanne and Galliard** (see page 74-76)
Branles (see page 77f)
a. **Simple**
b. **Washerwoman**
c. **Pease and Cog**
d. **Official**
e. **Gay**

Much laughing and conversation take place during many of the dances. (Remember, they are entertaining themselves.)

DIRECTOR

My Lord! We know that within this company there are many skilled in the intricate patterns of the Buffens Dance. We are prepared to provide the tune should there be those willing to execute the steps!

"Yes, yes!" from the lords and ladies. Four dancers emerge from the group, and the STEWARD *provides them with belts and swords,* The Buffens Dance *follows. It is difficult, macho, and often dangerous because of the wielding of swords. Much "oohing" and "aahing," especially from the ladies, is appropriate.*

LORD 7.
Will our Lord and Lady favor us with a special dance of their own choice?

ALL.
Yes, Yes!

LORD PHILLIP *upon conferring with his Lady.*
Musicians! Let us have LaVolta!

The LaVolta *follows. It is a duet dance which is flamboyant and difficult. The dancers must be strong and agile, and should be wearing the finest and sturdiest of costumes.*

LORD PHILLIP.
Dear musicians, let us now have a time of relaxation, and an opportunity to catch our breath with a gentle pavanne.

MUSIC: **Pavanne** (see page 74)

LADY BARBARA.
In truth, such beautiful music and dancing does exhaust our spirits. This evening of high festivity has begun to make me anticipate the pleasures of repose and sleep. Let us recall the slumber of the infant King who dozed beneath Mary's loving gaze and Joseph's protective presence on a clear night long ago.

MUSIC: **Sweet Was the Song** (see page 50)
Lullaby (Galaxy Music Corp.)

House lights dim as the STEWARD *gives each Lord and Lady a large lit candle, while* LORD PHILLIP *speaks:*

LORD PHILLIP.
My Lords and Ladies and Noble Guests: we must now take leave of this hall and seek repose in our chambers. We shall look forward to seeing you all on the morrow. As we take our leave, let us sing of this holy season of Christmas which makes all England glad, provides us with pleasures for our senses to enjoy, and renews friendships which our hearts will forever treasure.

May the sights and sounds of this night fill all of us with the joy and peace of this holy season.

MUSIC: **Josef, lieber Josef mein** (see page 43)
Carol of Beauty (Oxford Book of Carols)

The lords and ladies leave the hall with their candles. They continue singing and slowly walk away through the hall entrances until they are no longer seen or heard.

This quiet and dramatic ending produces a great emotional hush after so much activity. There may be an intensely moving period of silence before applause begins and the performers return for their bows.

PART I

MUSIC FOR SINGERS WITH PLAYERS

The music in this section provides the traditional carols used in every madrigal dinner, *The Wassail Carol*, *The Boar's Head*, and *The Flaming Pudding Carol*. The other songs fit into the two scripts. The instrumental parts are of particular importance as they blend with the voices, or contrast with them, to add color and authenticity.

In performing this music the singer should project the message of the songs with clarity and enthusiasm. Strophic songs such as *The Wassail Carol* and *The Boar's Head Carol* should be performed with variety, e.g., soloist and instruments, chorus with singers and instruments, unison chorus, or instruments alone.

All dynamic markings, tempo indications, articulation marks, and assignment of unspecified voice parts are editorial suggestions. In some pieces bar lines have been added by the editor. Instruments may be employed to double voice parts or to take the place of singers on some parts. Set I of the instrumental parts includes many optional parts for performance with the singers. A cappella performances of some selections is desirable for a contrast of textures. Finger cymbals or small drums may be used to emphasize the rhythm in certain songs. The music has been arranged in the order of events, i.e., the procession carol *Nowell Sing We* is the first song.

Good taste is the guide in assigning instrumental forces to accentuate the mood of each composition.

Nowell Sing We

EARLY ENGLISH CAROL
Edited by John Haberlen

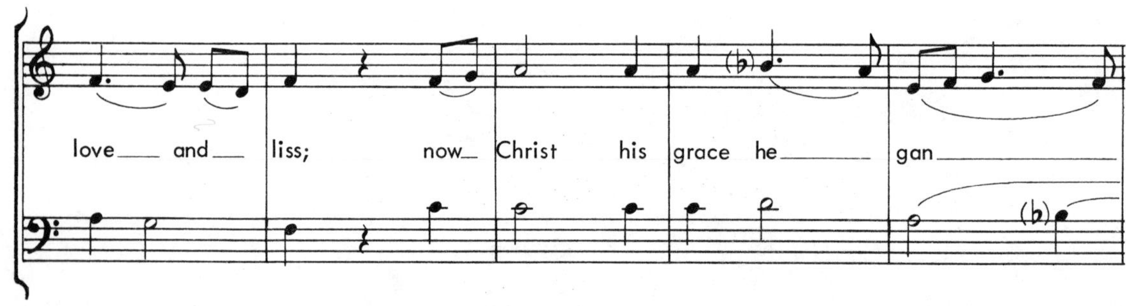

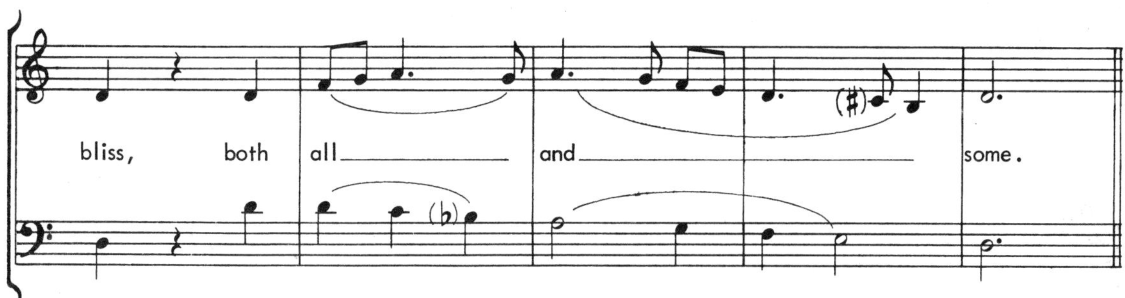

2. De fructu ventris of Mary bright;
Both God and man in her alight;
Out of disease he did us dight,
Both all and some.

3. Puer natus to us was sent,
To bliss us brought, fro bale us blent,
And else to woe we had y-went,
Both all and some.

4. Lux fulgebit with love and light,
In Mary mild his pynon pight,
In her took kind with manly might,
Both all and some.

5. Gloria tibi ay and bliss:
God unto his grace he us wiss,
The rent of heaven that we not miss,
Both all and some.

The Holly and the Ivy

TRADITIONAL ENGLISH CAROL
Arranged by Charles Knox

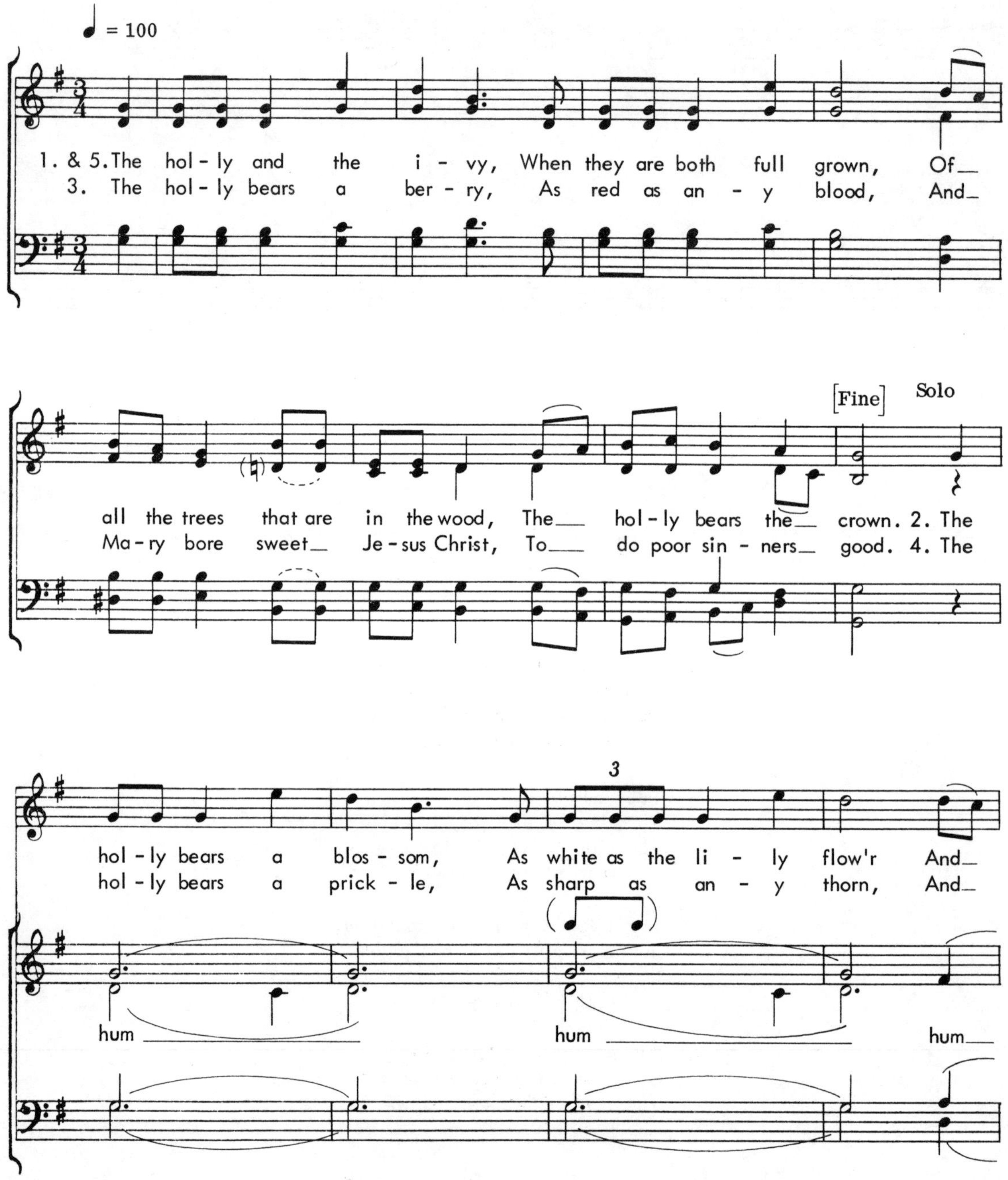

♩ = 100

1. & 5. The hol - ly and the i - vy, When they are both full grown, Of_
3. The hol - ly bears a ber - ry, As red as an - y blood, And_

[Fine] Solo

all the trees that are in the wood, The_ hol - ly bears the_ crown. 2. The
Ma - ry bore sweet_ Je - sus Christ, To_ do poor sin - ners_ good. 4. The

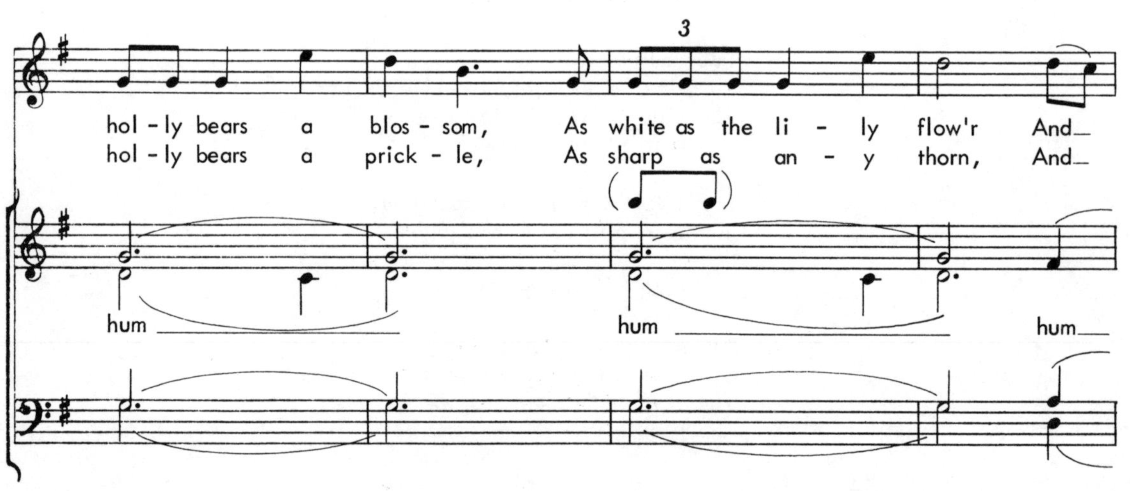

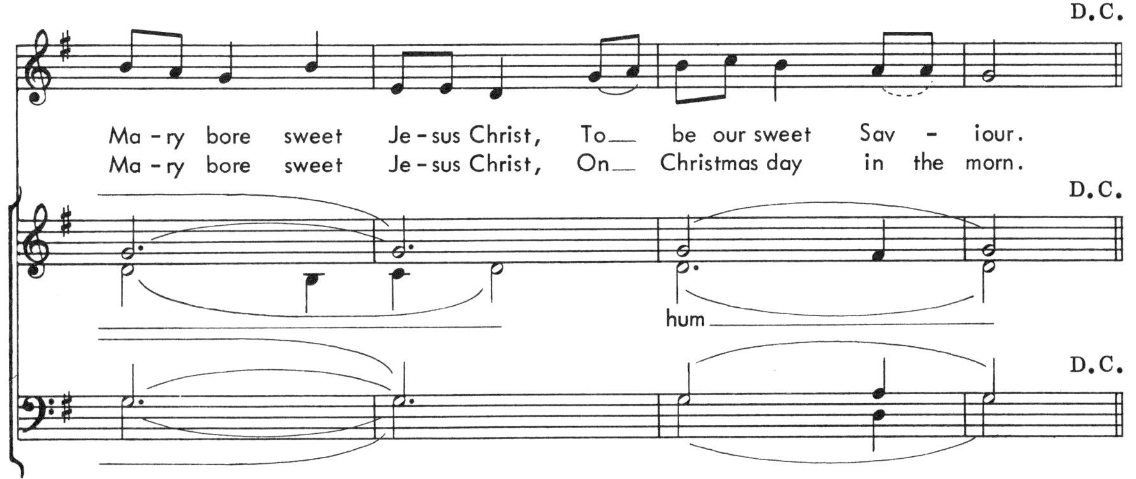

1. The holly and the ivy,
When they are both full grown,
Of all the trees that are in the wood,
The holly bears the crown.

2. The holly bears a blossom,
As white as the lily flower,
And Mary bore sweet Jesus Christ,
To be our sweet Saviour.

3. The holly bears a berry,
As red as any blood,
And Mary bore sweet Jesus Christ
To do poor sinners good.

4. The holly bears a prickle,
As sharp as any thorn,
And Mary bore sweet Jesus Christ
On Christmas day in the morn.

5. The holly and the ivy,
When they are both full grown,
Of all the trees that are in the wood,
The holly bears the crown.

Green Grow'th the Holly

HENRY VIII
Edited by John Haberlen

BURDEN 𝅗𝅥 = 72

VERSES (To be spoken)

1. As the holly grow'th green
   And never changeth hew
   So I am, ever hath been
   Unto my lady true.

2. As the holly grow'th green
   With ivy all alone,
   When flowers cannot be seen
   And greenwood leaves be gone.

3. Now unto my lady
   Promise to her I make,
   From all other only
   To her I me betake.

4. Adieu, mine own lady,
   Adieu, my special,
   Who hath my heart truly,
   Be sure, and ever shall.

Wassail Song

TRADITIONAL CAROL
Arranged by Charles Knox

1. Wassail, wassail, all over the town!
Our toast it is white, and our ale it is brown,
Our bowl it is made of the white maple tree;
With the wassailing bowl we'll drink to thee.

2. So here is to Cherry and to his right cheek,
Pray God send our master a good piece of beef,
And a good piece of beef that may we all see;
With the wassailing bowl we'll drink to thee.

3. And here is to Dobbin and to his right eye,
Pray God send our master a good Christmas pie,
And a good Christmas pie that may we all see;
With our wassailing bowl we'll drink to thee.

4. So here is to Broad May and to her broad horn,
May God send our master a good crop of corn,
And a good crop of corn that may we all see;
With the wassailing bowl we'll drink to thee.

5. And here is to Fillpail and to her left ear,
Pray God send our master a happy New Year,
And a happy New Year as e'er he did see;
With our wassailing bowl we'll drink to thee.

6. And here is to Colly and to her long tail,
Pray God send our master he never may fail
A bowl of strong beer; I pray you draw near,
And our jolly wassail it's then you shall hear.

7. Come, butler, come fill us a bowl of the best,
Then we hope that your soul in heaven may rest;
But if you do draw us a bowl of the small,
Then down shall go butler, bowl and all.

8. Then here's to the maid in the lily white smock,
Who tripped to the door and slipped back the lock!
Who tripped to the door and pulled back the pin,
For to let these jolly wassailers in.

The Boar's Head Carol

TRADITIONAL ENGLISH
Edited and Arranged by John Haberlen

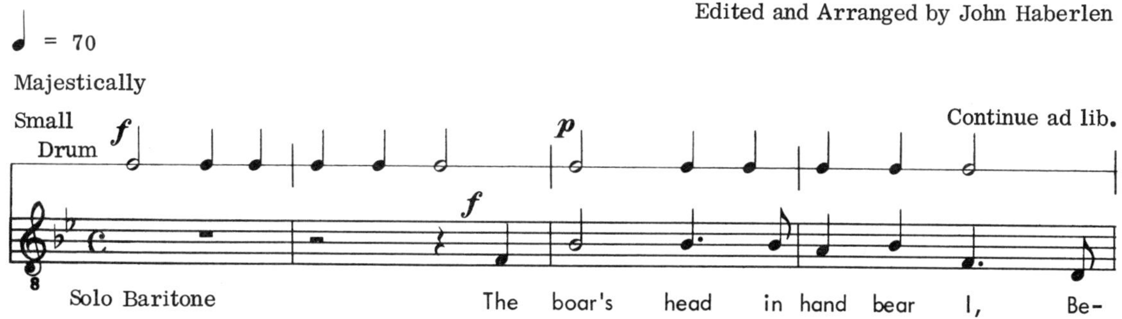

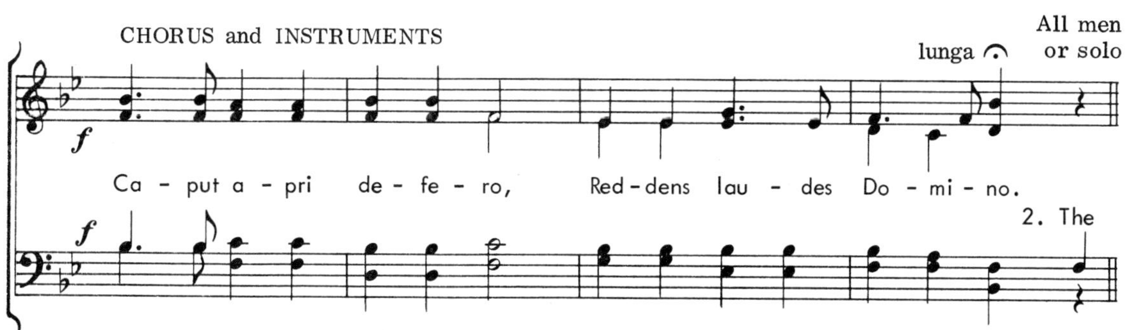

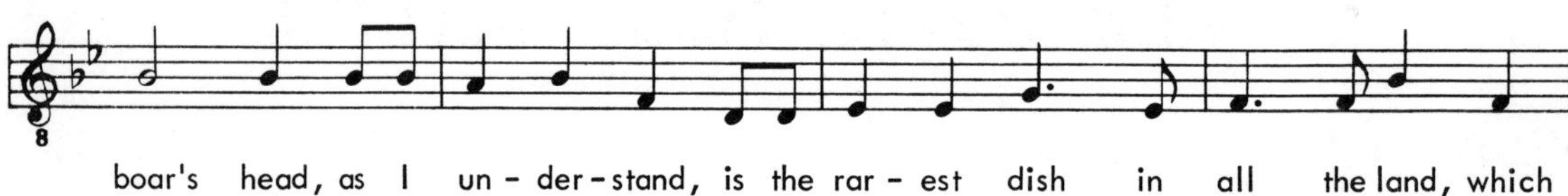

boar's head, as I un - der - stand, is the rar - est dish in all the land, which

Repeat the Chorus

thus be-decked with a gay gar - land, Let us ser - vi - re can - ti - co.

Unison voices or solo

3. Our stew - ard hath pro-vid - ed this, in hon-our of the King of Bliss, which

Repeat the Chorus twice

on this day to be serv - ed is, In Re - gin - en - si a - tri -o.

OPTIONAL STANZAS

1. A boar is a sovereign beast
Acceptable in ev'ry feast;
So mote this Lord be to most and least;
Nowell, nowell, nowell, nowell:

2. This boar's head we bring with song
In worship of him that thus sprang
Of a virgin to redress all wrong;
Nowell, nowell, nowell, nowell.

The Flaming Pudding Carol

TRADITIONAL
Arranged by John Haberlen
and James McKelvy

B
Come__ bring__ with a noise,__ my__ mer - ry mer - ry boys, the__
Christ - mas pud - ding a - flam - ing while my good dame she bids ye
all__ be__ free and__ eat to your heart's de - sir - ing!
C
8
Come__ bring__ with a noise, my__ mer - ry mer - ry boys, the__
8
Christ - mas__ pud - ding a - flam - ing while my good__ dame__ she__ bids ye

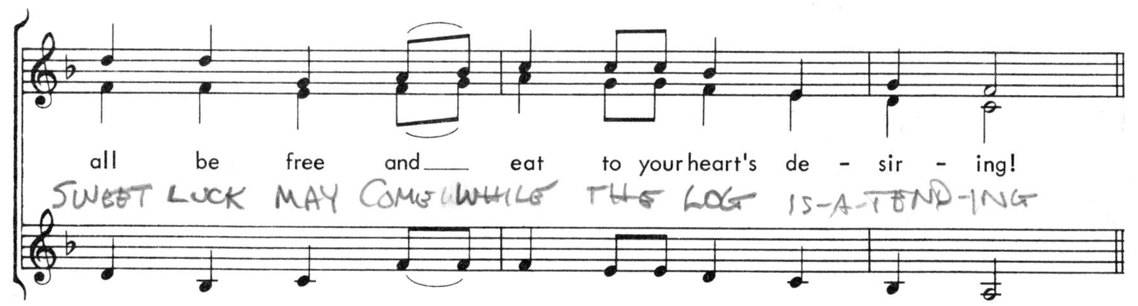

OPTIONAL AT B

With the last year's brand,
Light the new block, and
For good success in his spending
On your psalteries play,
That sweet luck may
Come while the log is a tending.

OPTIONAL AT C

Drink now the strong beer,
Cut the white loaf here;
The while the meat is a shredding
For the rare mince pie,
And the plums stand by
To fill the paste that's a kneading.

An Earthly Tree, a Heavenly Fruit

WILLIAM BYRD
Edited by John Haberlen

all.
From drow - sy sleep, that made old A - dam
And by his fault gave to man - kind his
weep,
fall. For lo! This day, the birth - day, day of
For lo! This day, the birth - day, day of
p
p
p

mp
days,
sum – mons our songs,
mp
days,
sum – mons our songs,
sum – mons our
mp
sum – mons our songs
mf
to give Him
mf
songs
to give Him laud
and praise,
mf
f
laud
and praise,
to give Him laud
and praise.
f
to give Him laud
and praise.
f

Cast Off All Doubtful Care

WILLIAM BYRD
Edited by John Haberlen

tears, to joy - ful news di - vine, di - vine, to
tears, to joy - ful news di - - - -
tears, to joy - ful news di - vine, news di - vine,
tears, to joy - ful

joy - ful news di - vine, di - vine, to joy - ful news di -
vine, to joy - ful news di - vine, to joy - ful
to joy - ful news di - vine,
news di - vine, to joy - ful news di - vine, to

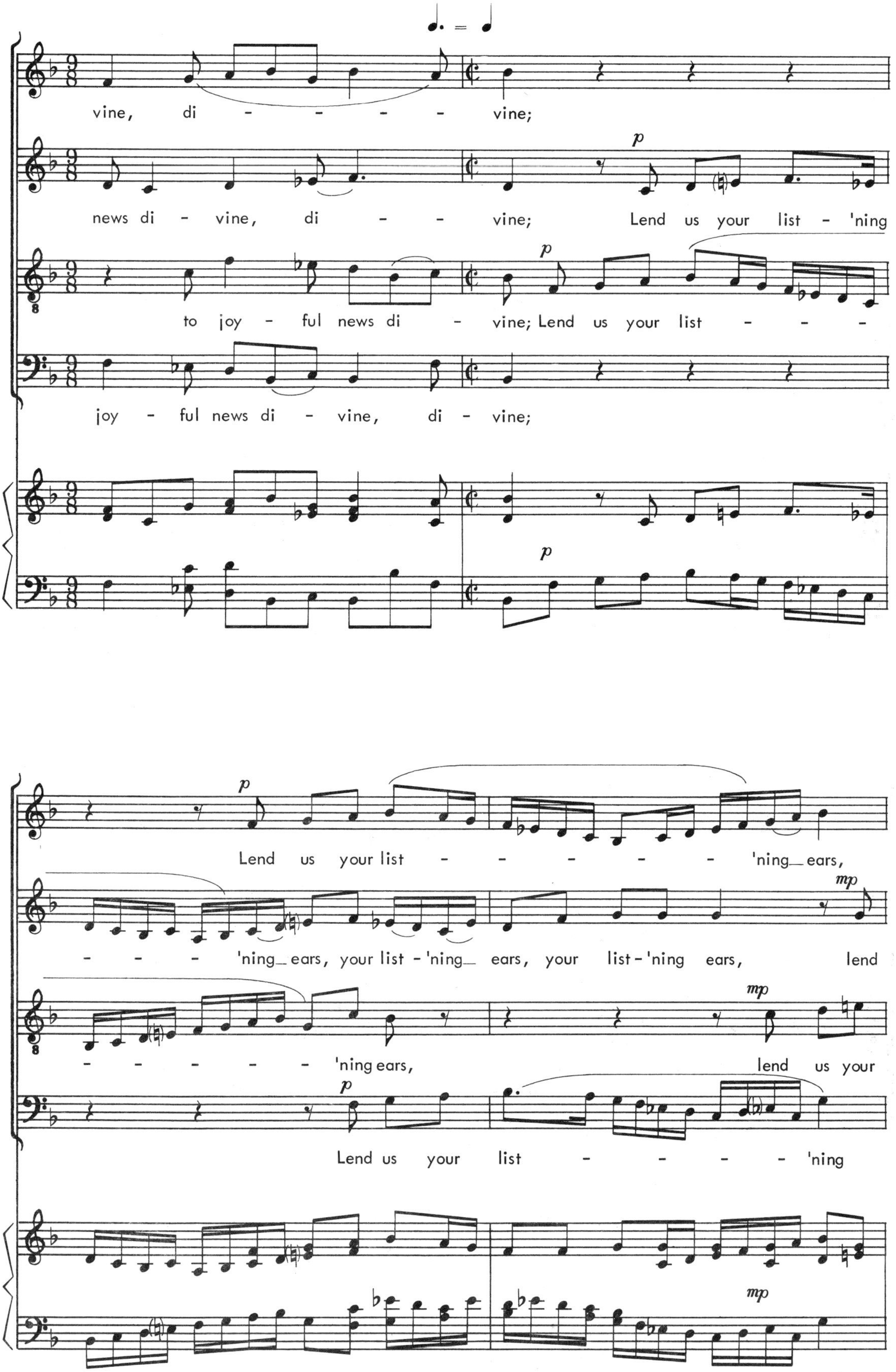
vine, di - - - - - vine;
p
news di - vine, di - - - vine; Lend us your list - 'ning
p
to joy - ful news di - vine; Lend us your list - - -
joy - ful news di - vine, di - vine;
p
p
Lend us your list - - - - - 'ning ears,
mp
- - - 'ning ears, your list - 'ning ears, your list - 'ning ears, lend
mp
- - - - - 'ning ears, lend us your
p
Lend us your list - - - - 'ning
mp

mp
lend us your list - - 'ning_ ears,
mf
us your list - - - - - - - - 'ning ears, lend
list - - - - 'ning ears, lend us your list - - -
mp
ears, your list -'ning ears,
mf

mf
lend us your list - - - - - - -
f
us your list - - 'ning ears, lend us your list - - 'ning_ ears, lend
mf
f
- 'ning ears, your list - 'ning ears, list - 'ning_ ears,__ your list - -
mf
f
lend us your list - - 'ning ears, your list - -
f

f
- - 'ning ears, lend us your list - - 'ning ears.
ff
us your list - - - - 'ning ears, your list-'ning ears.
ff
- - 'ning ears, lend us your list - - - - 'ning ears.
f
ff
'ning ears, list-'ning ears, lend us your list-'ning ears.
ff

Allon, Gay Bergeres

A
mp
Suy-vez moy. Al-lon, allon voir le Roy, Qui du ciel, qui du ciel, en ter - re est
vez moy. Al-lon, allon voir le Roy, Qui du ciel en ter - re est nay, gay,
Suy-vez moy. Al-lon, al-lon voir le Roy, Qui du ciel, en ter - re est
Suy-vez moy.
A
mp
mf
nay. Gay, gay. Al - lon, gay, gay, gay Ber - ge - res, al - lon, gay,
gay, gay, gay. Al - lon, gay, gay, gay Ber - ge - res, al - lon, gay,
nay. Gay, gay. Al - lon, gay, gay, gay Ber - ge - res, al - lon, gay,
Al - lon, gay, gay, gay Ber - ge - res, al - lon, gay,
mf

B
mp
Al - lon, gay, soy - ez le - ge - res, Suy - vez moy. Un beau pre-sent
Al - lon, gay, soy - ez le - ge - res, Suy - vez moy. Un beau pre - sent
mp
Al - lon, gay, soy - ez le - ge-res, Suy - vez moy. Un beau pre - sent luy
Al - lon, gay, soy - ez le - ge - res, Suy - vez moy.
B
mp
luy fe - ray. De ce fla - go - let que j'ay, que j'ay tant gay.
luy fe - ray; de quoy? De ce fla - go - let que j'ay, que j'ay tant gay.
fe - ray; de quoy? De ce fla - go - let que j'ay, que j'ay tant gay.
de quoy?

mf
Al - lon, gay, gay, gay Ber - ge - res, al - lon, gay, Al - lon, gay, soy -
ez le - ge - res, Suy - vez moy. Un ga - steau luy don - ne - ray, un gasteau luy
ez le - ge - res, Suy - vez moy. Un gasteau luy don-neray, luy
ez le - geres, Suy - vez moy. Un ga-steau luy don -
ez le - ge - res, Suy - vez moy.
C
mp

mf
don - ne - ray;
Gay, gay.
mf
don - ne-ray; Et moy, Plain Ha-nap luy of-fri - ray. Gay, gay.
mf
f
- ne - ray; Et moy, Plain Ha-nap luy of-fri - ray. Gay, gay. Al-
mf
Et moy, Plain Ha-nap luy of - fri - ray. Gay, gay.
mf
f
f
Al - lon, gay, gay, gay Ber - ge - res, al - lon, gay, Al - lon, gay, soy -
f
Al - lon, gay, gay, gay Ber - ge- res, al - lon, gay, Al - lon, gay, soy -
- lon, gay, gay, gay Ber - ge - res, al - lon, gay, Al - lon, gay, soy -
f
Al - lon, gay, gay, gay Ber - ge - res, al - lon, gay, Al - lon, gay, soy -

D
ez le - ge - res, Suy- vez moy. Ho, ho, Paix - la,
ez le - ge-res, Suy - vez moy. Ho, ho, Paix -
ez le - ge - res, Suy- vez moy. Ho, ho, Paix - la,
ez le - ge - res, Suy- vez moy. Ho, ho, Paix - la, paix -
D
paix - la! Je le voy; Il tet-te bien sans le doigt, Il tet-te bien sans le
paix - la! Je le voy, je le voy; Il tet - te bien, il tet - te bien sans le doigt, sans le
paix - la! Je le voy, je le voy; Il tet-te bien sans le doigt, Il tet-te bien sans le
paix-la! Je le voy, je le voy; Il tet - te bien sans le

f
doigt, le pe-tit Roy, Gay, gay. Al - lon, gay, gay, gay Ber - ge - res, al - lon, gay,
f
doigt, le pe-tit Roy, Gay, gay. Al - lon, gay, gay, gay Ber - ge - res, al - lon, gay,
f
doigt, le pe-tit Roy. Al - lon, gay, gay, gay Ber - ge - res, al - lon, gay,
f
doigt, le pe-tit Roy. Al - lon, gay, gay, gay Ber - ge - res, al - lon, gay,
f
cresc.
rit.
Al - lon, gay, soy - ez le - ge - res, Le Roy boit, le Roy boit.
cresc.
rit.
Al - lon, gay, soy - ez le - ge-res, Le Roy boit, le Roy boit.
cresc.
rit.
Al - lon, gay, soy - ez le - ge-res, Le Roy boit, le Roy boit.
cresc.
rit.
Al - lon, gay, soy - ez le - ge - res, Le Roy boit, le Roy boit.
cresc.
rit.

Josef, lieber Josef mein

Joseph, Dearest Joseph Mild

English translation by Margita Haberlen

LEONART SCHRÖTER
(1540-1595)
With additions by James McKelvy

mf Tutti
ri - a, Ei - - a, ei - - a! Vir - go De - um
mf Tutti
ri - a, Ei - - a, Ei - - a! Vir - go De - um
Tutti mf
Ei - - a, Ei - - a! Vir - go De - um
mf Tutti
Ei - a, Ei - a! Vir - go De - um
mf
ge - nu - it, quem di-vi - na vo - lu-it cle-men - ti-a.
ge-nu - it, quem di-vi - na vo - lu-it cle-men - ti-a.
ge - nu - it, quem di-vi - na vo - lu-it cle-men - ti-a.
ge - nu - it, quem di-vi - na vo - lu-it cle-men - ti-a.

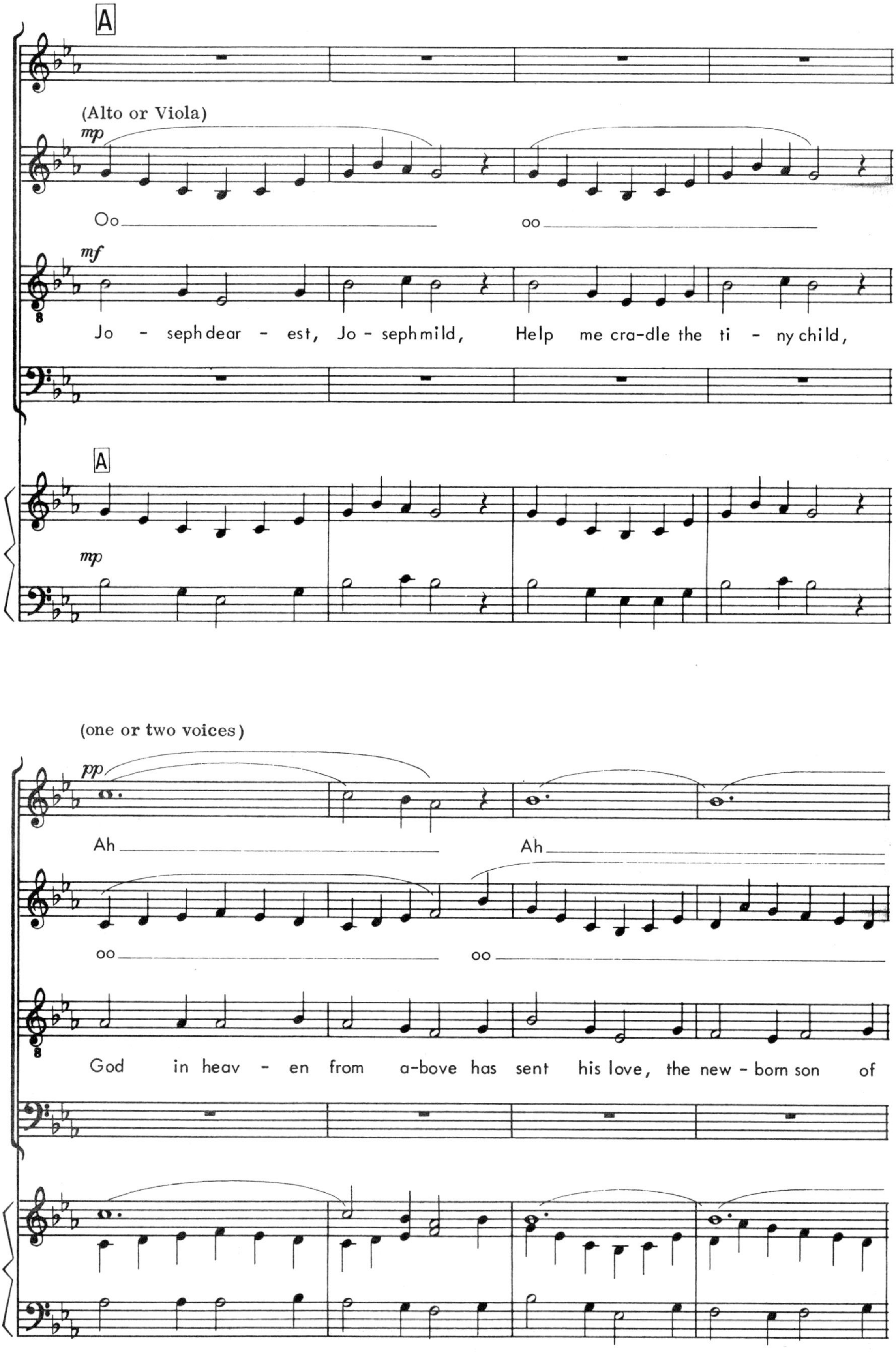

A

(Alto or Viola)

mp

Oo

oo

mf

Jo - seph dear - est, Jo - seph mild, Help me cra-dle the ti - ny child,

A

mp

(one or two voices)

mf Tutti
Ei - a, Ei - a, Vir - go De - um
mf Tutti
Ei - - a, Ei - - a, Vir - go De - um
mf Tutti
Ma - ry. Ei - - a, Ei - - a, Vir - go De - um
mf Tutti
Ei - a, Ei - a, Vir - go De - um
mf
ge - nu - it, quem di - vi - na vo - lu - it cle - men - ti - a.
ge - nu - it, quem di - vi - na vo - lu - it cle - men - ti - a.
ge - nu - it, quem di - vi - na vo - lu - it cle - men - ti - a.
ge - nu - it, quem di - vi - na vo - lu - it cle - men - ti - a.

B
mf
Let the harp with psal - ter ring, prais - es to the gen - tle King,
mf
Let the harp with psal - ter ring, prais - es to the gen - tle King,
f
Let the harp with psal - ter ring, prais - es to the gen - tle King,
mf
Let the harp with psal - ter ring, prais - es to the gen - tle King,
B
mf
dim.
Raise your voic - es all in one to glo - ri - fy the birth of Christ, the
Raise your voic - es all in one to glo - ri - fy the birth of Christ,
Raise your voic - es all in one to glo - ri - fy the birth of Christ,
Raise your voic - es all in one to glo - ri - fy the birth of Christ,

pp
in - fant son. Ei - a, ei - a,
dim.
p
in - fant son. Ei - - a, ei - - a,
dim.
pp
in - fant son. Ei - - a, ei - - a,
dim.
p
in - fant son. Ei - a, ei - - a,
dim.
p
C
f
Christ the Lord is born to-day, is born to-day in
f
Christ the Lord is born, born to-day, is born to-day in
f
Christ the Lord is born, born to-day, is born to-day in
f
Christ the Lord is born, is born to-day, is born to-day in
C
f

Is - ra - el, As fore - told by Gab - ri - el. Al-
Is - ra - el, As fore - told by Gab - ri - el. Al-
Is - ra - el, As fore - told by Gab - ri - el. Al-
Is - ra - el, As fore - told by Gab - ri - el. Al-
le - - - lu - ia.
le - lu - ia, Al - le - lu - ia.
le - - - lu - ia, Al - le - lu - ia.
le - - - lu - ia, Al - le - lu - ia.

Sweet Was the Song the Virgin Sang

ANONYMOUS
Keyboard Realization by Charles Knox
Edited by John Haberlen

li - ver'd of her Son, That bless - ed Je - sus hath to name.
Lul - la, lul - la, lul - la, lul - la - by, lul - la, lul - la, lul - la, lul - la - by, Sweet

Babe, quoth— she, My son and eke a Sav - iour born,
mf
which hath vouch - saf - ed from on high To vis - it us that

were for - lorn. Lul - lul - la, lul - lul - la, lul - lul - la -
Ritard second time
Ritard second time
by. Sweet Babe, quoth she, And rock'd him feat - ly on her knee.

Pastime With Good Company

HENRY VIII

Youth must have some dalliance,
Of good or ill some pastance;
Company methinks then best
All thoughts and fancies to digest,
For idleness
Is chief mistress
Of vices all:
Then who can say
But mirth and play
Is best of all?

Company with honesty
Is virtue, vices to flee;
Company is good and ill,
But every man hath his free will.
The best ensue,
The worst eschew,
My mind shall be;
Virtue to use,
Vice to refuse,
Thus shall I use me.

Es ist ein' Ros'

Lo, How a Rose E'er Blooming

Angelus ad Virginem

PERFORMANCE NOTES

This carol was originally a sequence, and very popular in the Middle Ages, The two versions here were edited from facsimiles of the original manuscripts, found in "Early English Harmony" by the Reverend H.V. Hughes. The original Middle English has been harmonized and the pitch level of the music raised a fourth. Accidentals in parenthesis have been added to assure the pitch of the following note. The editor's suggestions of percussion, drones, and other instrumental parts are given in accordance with accepted Medieval performance practice. The conductor is free to use these added parts at his discretion.

The two versions can be used in alternation with various combinations of voices, instruments, and Latin stanzas. One possibility: Stanza one in unison, stanza two with a T T B semi-chorus, stanza three with an SSA semi-chorus, and stanza four again in unison.

The accidentals in the alto part in measures 25, 32 (second note), 34, 37, 38, and 41 have been added and are strongly suggested by the editor. The instruments indicated at the beginning of the score are simply suggestions. It would be inappropriate to use them all.

DENNIS MARTIN

Angelus ad Virginem

Text and Music
Medieval Anonymous

Edited and Arranged by
DENNIS MARTIN

SSA or TTB with selected instruments, recorders, woodwinds, strings.

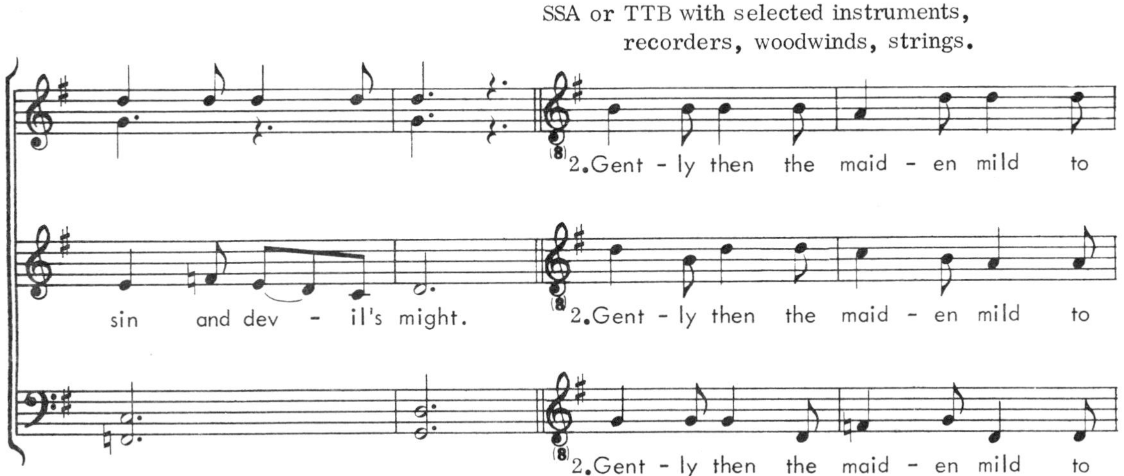

an - swer him be - gan - ne: "How shall I con - ceive a child, a
an - swer him be - gan - ne: "How shall I con - ceive a child, a
an - swer him be - gan - ne: "How shall I con - ceive a child, a

maid with - out a man - - - në?" Then said the
maid with - out a man - - - në?" Then said the
maid with - out a man - - - në?" Then said the

an - gel: "Fear thou naught; by th'Ho - ly Ghost it shall be wrought, This
an - gel: "Fear thou naught; by th'Ho - ly Ghost it shall be wrought, This
an - gel: "Fear thou naught; by th'Ho - ly Ghost it shall be wrought, This

3. When the maiden understood the word the angel toldë,
Mildly she, in gentle mood, her answer did unfoldë:
"Handmaiden of the Lord I wis, am I that have been raised to this;
Within my breast God's high behest is criéd since now I know it is
His will that maid unmarried shall have a mother's bliss."

4. Th' angel went away anon and vanished from her sightë,
And her womb did stir full through the Holy Ghost his mightë.
In her the seed of Christ was sown; true God, true man in flesh and bone,
Who born of her did flesh become to save us. Through him our hope is won,
Since on the cross he gave us his life to free our own.

5. Maiden mother, matchless one, with milk thy bosom filléd,
Ask our mercy of your son, till our worst fears be stilléd.
That he forgave us sin and pain, and of ev'ry guilt he make us clean,
And grant us bliss when our time is for dying. With life above to win
Here with God's will complying, that he will take us in.

Shepherds Rejoice

Text by J.H.

THOMAS MORLEY (1557-1603)
Edited and Arranged by JOHN HABERLEN
from "Ho! Who comes here?" (1594)

p legato
in the cat - tle shed the boy lies a-sleep, in the
mp legato
in the cat - tle shed a - sleep - ing,
cat - tle shed the ba - by boy is sleep - ing, is
pp legato
in the cat - tle shed, in the shed a
pp
poco staccato
f
cat - tle shed the boy lies sleep - ing; shep - herds re -
p
in the shed the boy lies sleep - ing;
p
sleep - ing, the boy lies sleep - ing;
p
boy lies sleep - - - ing;
f

A
joice on this day, re - joice on this day with bag - pip - ing and drum - ming, with
f poco staccato
shep - herds re - joice on this day with bag - pip - ing and drum - ming, with
f poco staccato
f
shep - herds re - joice! On this day re - joic - ing, with
poco staccato
f
with
A
bag - piping and drum - ming; in the cat - tle shed the
p legato
mp legato
bag - piping and drum - ming; in the cat - tle shed a -
p legato
bag - piping and drum - ming; in the cat - tle shed the ba - by boy is
mp legato
bag - piping and drum - ming; in the cat - tle shed, in the
p

pp
boy lies a-sleep, in the cat - tle shed the boy lies sleep - ing;
p
sleep - ing, in the shed the boy lies sleep - ing;
p
mf
sleep - ing, is sleep-ing, the boy lies sleep - ing; Come
p
mf
shed a boy lies sleep - - ing; Come
pp
mf
B
mf
Come, come, shep - herds, come
mf
Come, shep - herds, come quick - ly, come
shep - herds, quick - - ly, come, shep - herds,
shep - herds, come, come, shep - herds, come quick - ly,
B

shep - herds, come, come see the Sav - ior on
shep - herds, shep - herds, come, see the Sav - ior to-day on
come, come quick - ly, see Him on
come, shep - herds, come, come see the Sav - ior on
C
p
fresh - ly mown hay; No - el sing we, Fa la la
p
fresh - ly mown hay; No - el sing we, Fa
mp
fresh - ly mown hay; No - el sing we, Fa la la la la, Fa la la la
mp
fresh - ly mown hay; No - el sing we, Fa la, Fa la la
C
mp

la, Fa la la la la la la, No - el sing we, Fa la la
la, Fa la la la la la la, No - el sing we, Fa
la la, No - el sing we, Fa la la la la, Fa la la
la la, No - el sing we, Fa la la la, Fa
f
p
mf
1.
2.
la, Fa la la. la.
la la la, Fa la la. la.
la, Fa la la la la la la. Come la.
la la la la. Come la.

PART II

MUSIC FOR PLAYERS AND DANCERS

The Dance

Elizabethan dancing adds a thrilling dimension to any dinner presentation. An Elizabethan education included instruction in social graces such as singing and dancing. These accomplishments were expected at the frequent *feaste*, and were exhibited with a grandeur befitting the age. Early dances ran the gamut from solemn ritual, as in the *Pavanne*, to the exciting virtuosic displays of the *Buffens Dance* and *La Volta.*

A skillful choreographer is needed to select and teach the steps. To use bibliographical resource materials on the early dances, one must be knowledgeable about dance styles and techniques. Close and constant collaboration is essential between the choreographer and the music director.

Ideally, the dances should be selected *after* assessing the physical stamina and grace of the singers. A regular allotment of rehearsal time devoted to exercise and basic dance steps will bring best results. Memorization of the steps must be completed early so the performers may communicate the exuberance of bodies engaged in purposeful play.

Well in advance of the performances, the dancers must rehearse extensively in costume. The initial incredulity and tittering at men in tights and slippers and women in 10 to 15 pound dresses will disappear as the dancers concentrate on erasing clumsiness caused by the unfamiliar dress. The result will be presence and bearing convincing to an audience.

Your own unique problems will be discovered in the course of preparation and rehearsal. Allow the problems to surface early enough that you will have time to eliminate them. By the performance, you will have developed a troupe of performers at once disciplined, confident, integrated, and enthusiastic. The key to success is advance preparation.

The Music

The music in this section is to be used in a functional manner both for the dances and as incidental music. This is the raw material ready for the director to orchestrate for the greatest practical use with the instruments and players available. When it is used for the dances it must be played rhythmically, and in the exact tempo the dancers require; however as background music during dinner, tempos and orchestration can be varied considerably.

To realize attractive orchestration, it is preferable to have early instruments such as recorders and krummhorns. The more available modern woodwinds and strings with light percussion may substitute. Drums and brass are appropriate for the fanfares, and a small harpsichord is the ideal keyboard instrument.

The scores in this book may be used by the conductor or accompanist. Percussion indications are included. Dancers may use them for rehearsals and for notating their dance routines. The wire-bound edition of *Elizabethan Madrigal Dinners* is preferable for production use.

The instrumental parts are printed separately in a large format with each of the upper three parts, soprano, alto, and tenor, provided in different keys appropriate for the various instruments that might be employed. The parts are labeled to correspond to the four vocal parts. The Set includes:

2 Soprano parts in C
1 Soprano part in Bb

2 Alto parts in C
1 Alto part in Bb

2 Tenor parts in C
1 Tenor part in F
1 Tenor part in Alto Clef

2 Bass parts in C

After the dances have been choreographed, the music should be adjusted by repeating phrases, or sections, or deleting them, depending upon the number of measures required. The conductor's score shows the number of measures in each section of music.

It is easier to dance with the steady beat of a small drum, tambourine, or finger cymbal than to the less rhythmic timbre of winds and strings. Consider having the conductor play the percussion instruments rather than lead with gestures. Then, with a few introductory measures of percussion, he will establish the right tempo for both the dancers and players.

The following are suggestions for assigning parts:

KEYBOARD
Harpsichord, Guitar, Harp, Portative Organ

SOPRANO in C
Recorder, Krummhorn, Violin, Flute, Oboe

SOPRANO in Bb
Clarinet, Trumpet

ALTO in C
Recorder, Krummhorn, Violin, Flute, Oboe

ALTO in Bb
Clarinet, Trumpet

TENOR in C
Recorder, Krumhorn, Cello, Trombone, Sackbut

TENOR in F
English Horn, French Horn

TENOR in ALTO CLEF
Viola

BASS in C
Recorder, Krummhorn, Cello, String Bass, Bassoon, Trombone, Sackbut

Instrumental combinations may be formed in instrumental families such as strings (Violin, Viola, Cello), or recorders (soprano, alto, teno, bass). Combinations of different instruments (called broken consorts) may lend more variety to the sound and be easier to assemble. Here are some possibilities:

WINDS
Soprano Recorder, Alto Recorder, Tenor Recorder, Alto Krummhorn

Soprano Recorder, Oboe, French Horn, Bassoon

Oboe, Clarinet, French Horn, Bassoon

STRINGS and WINDS
Violin, Oboe, Viola, Bassoon

Oboe, Violin, French Horn, Cello

Several different instruments of the same aproximate range can be assigned the same part, although this kind of doubling works best with good players.

The keyboard may be used to support weak parts or to supply missing ones; it will add a percussive quality especially appropriate for the dances; and it may be used as the accompaniment for solo instrumental or vocal numbers.

One must be creative in using available instruments and players, always with thought for accurate reproduction of the style.

The Fanfare

The fanfares given here are not authentic. Feel free to compose your own, taking into consideration the instruments you plan to use, the ability of the players, and their placement in the program.

Fanfares

#1 Based on a Lionel Power fragment

Arranged by
James McKelvy

#3 Based on a Medieval Anonymous setting of Angelus ad Virginem
Arranged by James McKelvy
poco rit.
poco rit.
#4 Based on Dufay's Trumpet Gloria
Arranged by James McKelvy
molto rit.
molto rit.
#5 A Madrigal Dinner Fanfare
John Haberlen
poco rit.
poco rit.

Pavane 1

PIERRE ATTAINGNANT
Edited and Arranged by
Stephen Rosolack

𝅗𝅥 (8+8) (8+8) (4+4) (8+8)

Pavane 2
THOINOT ARBEAU
Transcribed by
Stephen Rosolack
(8+8) (8+8)

Galliard

PIERRE ATTAINGNANT
Edited and Arranged by
Stephen Rosolack

Branle–Simple
PIERRE ATTAINGNANT
Edited and Arranged by
Stephen Rosolack
(6+6) (6+6)

Branle–Washerwoman

PIERRE ATTAINGNANT
Arranged by
Stephen Rosolack

Branle–Pease and Cog

THOINOT ARBEAU
Transcribed and Arranged by
Stephen Rosolack

Branle–Official

THOINOT ARBEAU
Transcribed and Arranged by
Stephen Rosolack

Branle–Gay

PIERRE ATTAINGNANT
Edited and Arranged by
Stephen Rosolack

Buffens

THOINOT ARBEAU
Transcribed and Arranged by
Stephen Rosolack

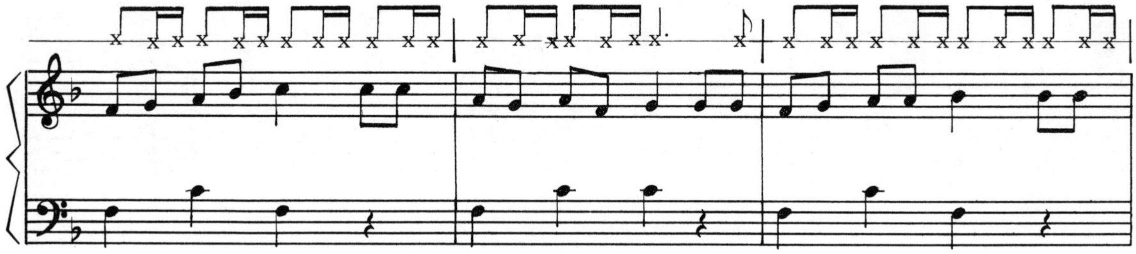

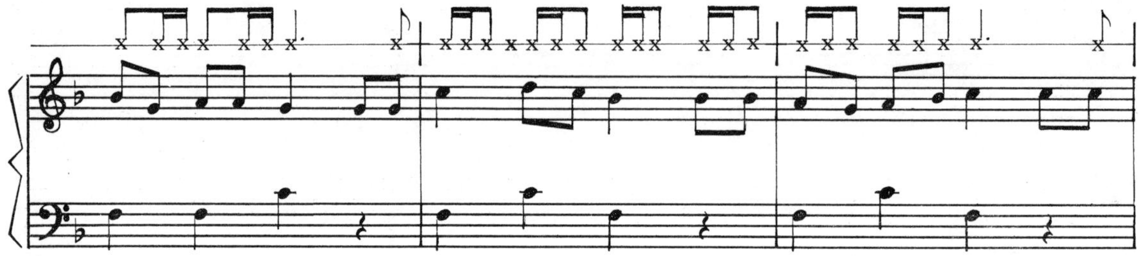

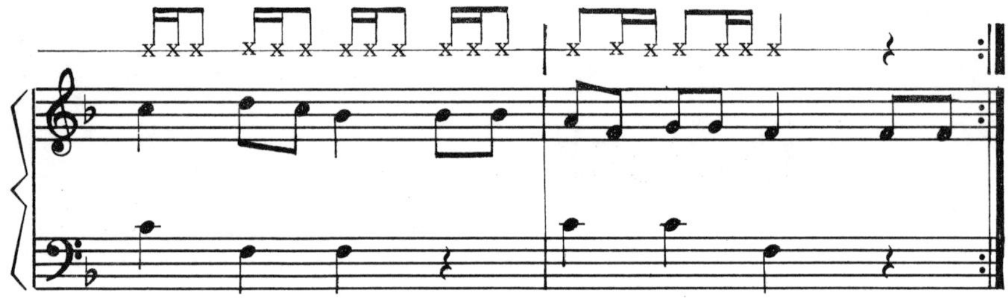

La Volta

WILLIAM BYRD
Edited and Arranged by
STEPHEN ROSOLACK

𝅗𝅥. (4+4) (4+4) (4+4) (4+4)

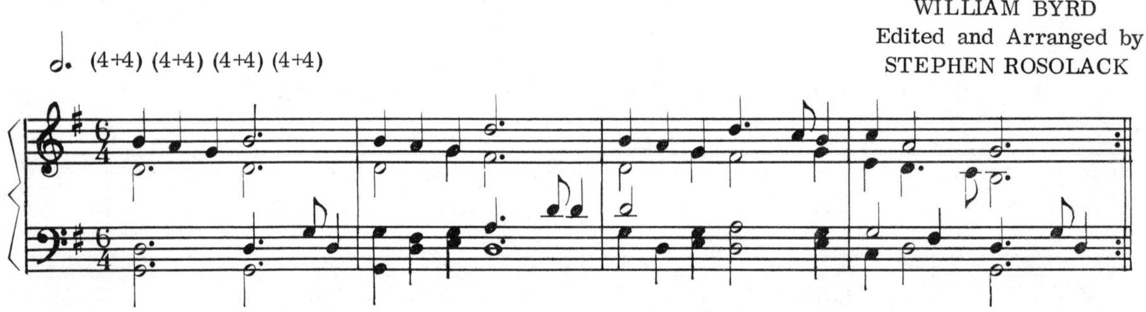

Basse Danse

PIERRE ATTAINGNANT
Edited and Arranged by
Stephen Rosolack

(16+16) (16+16)

PART III

MUSIC FOR SINGERS, PLAYERS, AND AUDIENCES

The familiar carol music in Part III is for audience participation, and for singers and players to perform before or during the dinner.

The two scripts specify that the audience is to join in the singing of *Deck the Halls, Joy to the World* and *O Come All Ye Faithful.* If it is desired to add the words or music to the printed program or to provide a brief song sheet, the purchaser of this book is hereby authorized to reprint such selections as are needed for that purpose. One may wish to substitute other carols for these script suggestions, or one may expand audience participation with additional carols.

For some presentations the singers, or a second group of singers, or players, may provide music for the people assembling for dinner but not yet invited into the main hall. For this, people appreciate familiar carols.

During the dinner the singers may divide into two groups to alternate carols from the far ends of the hall. Another possibility is a strolling quartet. Stanzas of carols not included here may be found in the *Oxford Book of Carols.*

For instrumental background music, just as with the predinner music selections, the familiar carols are much appreciated. Music from Part III, when interspersed with the Renaissance dance music from Part II, will lend more variety.

The music in Part III is virtually unedited. Players and singers must plan tempos, dynamics, phrasing, and ornamentation. Directors must additionally be concerned with tonal variety and part balance as they select which instruments are to play which parts. All the instruments should not play all the time.

Remember, people talk while eating, so background music really must be kept in the background. Alternatives to the group of Renaissance instruments are the harpsichord or harp. To be avoided is the brass ensemble, which even at its softest, is too loud for nearby table conversation.

The incidental music of the evening should not be regarded lightly. Careful attention to the programming and rehearsing of this music will help your audience be more receptive to the main program.

Coventry Carol

Robert Croo, 1534

16th Century English Carol
Arranged by James McKelvy

A Lully, lullay, Thou little tiny Child,
Bye, bye, lully, lullay.

B O sisters, too how may we do,
For to preserve this day;
This poor Youngling for whome we sing,
Bye, bye, lully, lullay.

C Herod the king, is his raging,
Charged he hath this day;
His men of might, in his own sight,
All children young, to slay.

D Then woe is me, poor Child, for Thee,
And ever mourn and say;
For Thy parting nor say nor sing,
Bye, bye, ully, lullay.

E Lully, lullay, Thou little tiny Child,
Bye, bye, lully, lullay.

Away in a manger no crib for a bed,
The little Lord Jesus laid down His sweet head,
The stars in the sky, looked down where He lay,
The little Lord Jesus, asleep on the hay.

The cattle were lowing, the poor baby wakes,
But little Lord Jesus, no crying He makes,
I love Thee, Lord Jesus, look down from the sky,
And stay by my cradle, 'till morning is nigh.

Traditional Welsh Carol

Deck the hall with boughs of holly, Fa la la
'Tis the season to be jolly, Fa la la
Don we now our gay apparel, Fa la la
Troll the ancient Yuletide carol, Fa la la

See the blazing Yule before us, Fa la la
Strike the harp and join the chorus, Fa la la
Follow me in merry measure, Fa la la
While I tell of Yuletide treasure, Fa la la

The First Noel

16th Century, French

The first Noel the angels did say
Was to certain poor shepherds in fields as they lay:
In fields where they lay keeping their sheep
On a cold winter's night that was so deep.
Noel, Noel, Noel, Noel. Born is the King of Israel.

They looked up and saw a star
Shining in the east beyond them far,
And to the earth it gave great light.
And so it continued both day and night.
Noel, Noel, Noel, Noel. Born is the King of Israel.

And by the light of that same star,
Three Wisemen came from country far,
To seek for a King was their intent.
And to follow the star wherever it went.
Noel, Noel, Noel, Noel. Born is the King of Israel.

God Rest Ye Merry, Gentlemen

16th Century Swedish

God rest ye merry, gentlemen, Let nothing you dismay,
Remember Christ our Savior Was born on Christmas Day;
To save us all from Satan's pow'r, When we were gone astray.
O tidings of comfort and joy.

In Bethlehem, in Jewry, This blesses Babe was born,
And laid within a manger, Upon this blessed morn;
The which His Mother Mary, Did nothing take in scorn.
O tidings of . . .

From God our Heav'nly Father, A blessed Angel came;
And unto certain Shepherds, Brought tidings of the same:
How that in Bethlehem was born The Son of God by Name.
O tidings of . . .

The Shepherds at those tidings Rejoiced much in mind,
And left their flocks a-feeding, In tempest, storm, and wind:
And went to Bethlehem straightway, The Son of God to find.
O tidings of . . .

Good King Wenceslas

Old English Carol

Good King Wenceslas look'd out On the feast of Stephen,
When the snow lay round about, Deep and crisp and even;
Brightly shone the moon that night, Tho' the frost was cruel,
When a poor man came in sight, Gath'ring winter fuel.

"Hither, page, and stand by me, If thou know'st it, telling;
Yonder peasant, who is he? Where, and what his dwelling?"
"Sire, he lives a good league hence, Underneath the mountain;
Right against the forest fence, By Saint Agnes' fountain."

"Bring me flesh, and bring me wine, Bring me pinelogs hither;
Thou and I will see him dine When we bear them thither."
Page and monarch forth they went, Forth they went together;
Thro' the rude wind's wild lament And the bitter weather.

"Sire, the night is darker now, And the wind blows stronger;
Fails my heart, I know not how, I can go no longer."
"Mark my footsteps, my good page, Tread thou in them boldly:
Thou shalt find the winter's rage Freeze thy blood less coldly."

In his master's steps he trod, Where the snow lay dinted;
Heat was in the very sod Which the saint had printed;
Therefore, Christian men, be sure, Wealth or rank possessing,
Ye who now will bless the poor, Shall yourselves find blessing.

Hark! The Herald Angels Sing

Charles Wesley, 1739

Felix Mendelssohn, 1840
Arranged by James McKelvy

1. Hark! the herald angels sing,
"Glory to the newborn King!
Peace on earth, and mercy mild,
God and sinners reconciled."
Joyful, all ye nations, rise,
Join the triumph of the skies;
With th'angelic host proclaim,
Christ is born in Bethlehem."

2. Christ, by highest heav'n adored;
Christ, the everlasting Lord;
Late in time behold Him come,
Offspring of the favored one.
Veiled in flesh, the Godhead see;
Hail th' incarnate Deity
Pleased, as man with men to dwell,
Jesus, our Immanuel!

3. Hail! the heav'nborn Prince of Peace!
Hail! the Son of Righteousness!
Light and life to all He brings,
Ris'n with healing in His wings,
Mild He lays His glory by,
Born that man no more may die:
Born to raise the sons of earth,
Born to give them second birth.

Hark! the herald angels sing, "Glory to the newborn King!"

I Heard the Bells

Henry W. Longfellow, 1863 — J. Baptiste Calkin, 1872

1. I heard the bells on Christmas day
Their old familiar carols play,
And wild and sweet the words repeat
Of peace on earth, good will to men.

2. I thought how, as the day had come,
The belfries of all Christendom
Had roll'd along th'unbroken song
Of peace on earth, good will to men.

3. And in despair I bow'd my head:
"There is no peace on earth," I said
"For hate is strong, and mocks the song
Of peace on earth, good will to men."

4. Then pealed the bells more loud and deep:
"God is not dead, nor doth he sleep;
The wrong shall fail, the right prevail,
With peace on earth, good will to men."

I Saw Three Ships

15th Century English
Arranged by John Stainer

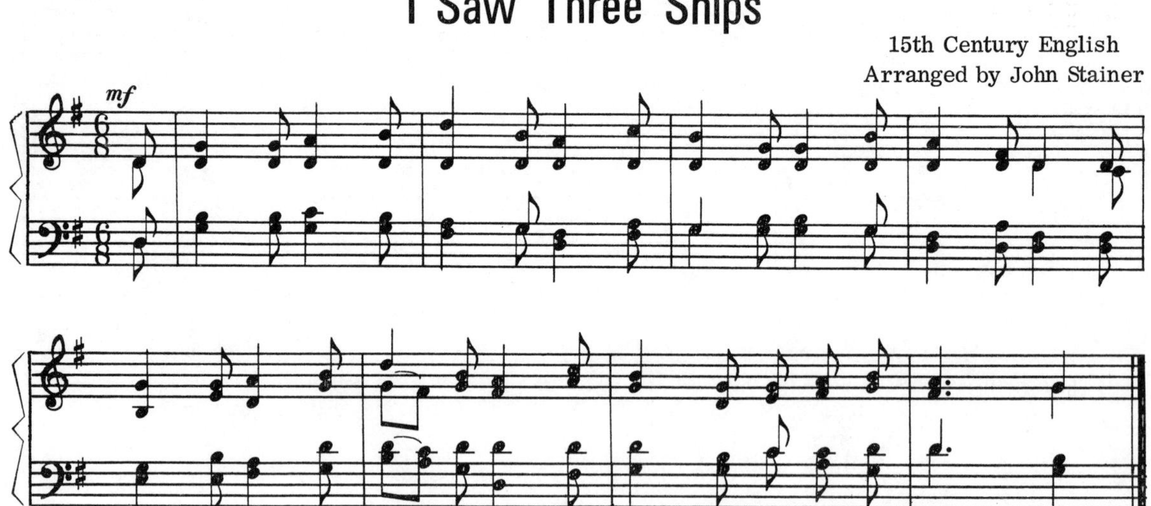

I saw three ships come sailing in.
On Christmas Day, on Christmas Day;
I saw three ships come sailing in,
On Christmas Day in the morning.

And what was in those ships all three,
On Christmas Day, on Christmas Day;
And what was in those ships all three,
On Christmas Day in the morning.

The Virgin Mary and Child were there,
On Christmas Day, on Christmas Day;
The Virgin Mary and Child were there,
On Christmas Day in the morning.

It Came Upon the Midnight Clear

Edmund H. Sears, 1850

Richard S. Willis, 1851

1. It came upon the midnight clear,
   That glorious song of old,
From angels bending near the earth,
   To touch their harps of gold;
"Peace on the earth, good will to men
   From heav'n's all gracious King,"
The world in solemn stillness lay
   To hear the angels sing.

2. Still thro' the cloven skies they come,
   With peaceful wings unfurled;
And still their heav'nly music floats
   O'er all the weary world:
Above its sad and lowly plains
   They bend on hov'ring wing,
And ever o'er its Babel sounds
   The blessed angels sing.

3. O ye beneath life's crushing load,
   Whose forms are bending low,
Who toil along the climbing way
   With painful steps and slow;
Look now, for glad and golden hours
   Come swiftly on the wing;
Oh rest beside the weary road
   And hear the angels sing.

4. For lo! the days are hast'ning on,
   By prophets seen of old,
When with the evercircling years
   Shall come the time foretold,
When the new heav'n and earth shall own
   The Prince of Peace the King,
And the whole world send back the song
   Which now the angels sing.

Jingle Bells Scherzo

As the measures change from 2-4 to 5-8, etc., an eighth note should equal an eighth note throughout. The tempo should not be too fast at the beginning, but it might increase slightly as the scherzo progresses.

Arranged by
JAMES McKELVY

Bells on bob - tail ring, Mak - ing spir - its bright; What
way; Bells on bob - tail ring, Mak-ing spir - its
fun it is to ride and sing a sleigh-ing song to - night, a
bright; What fun it is to ride and sing a sleigh-ing song to -
sleigh-ing song to - night! Jin - gle bells Oh Jin - gle bells Oh
night!
Jin - gle all the way! Oh what fun it is to ride in a
one-horse o-pen sleigh! Jin - gle bells Oh Jin - gle bells Oh
Jin - gle all the way! Oh what fun it is to ride in a

one-hors-y wide o-pen sleigh!
one-hors-y wide o-pen Jin - gle bells Oh Jin-gle bells Oh Jin - gle bells Oh
Jin - gle bells Oh Jin-gle bells Oh Jin - gle bells Oh

Oh what fun it
Jin - gle bells Oh Jin-gle all the way! Oh what fun what fun it

is to ride in a one - horse o - pen sleigh! Jin - gle bells Oh

Oh what fun it
Jin - gle bells Oh Jin - gle all the way! Oh what fun what fun it

mf
Jin - gle bells Oh
is to ride in a one-hors-y wide o-pen sleigh!
Jin - gle bells Oh

mp
Jin - gle bells Oh Jin - gle bells Oh Jin - gle bells Oh Jin - gle bells!
Jing! Jin - gle bells Oh Jin - gle bells Oh Jin- gle all the
mf
Jin - gle bells Oh Jin - gle bells Oh Jin - gle all the

Jin - gle bells! Jin - gle bells! Jin - gle bells! Jin - gle bells!
way! Oh what fun it is to ride in a one - horse o - pen
way! Oh what fun what fun it is to ride in a one - horse o - pen

Jin - gle bells! Jin - gle bells Oh Jin - gle bells Oh Jin - gle bells!
sleigh! Jin - gle bells Oh Jin - gle bells Oh Jin - gle all the
sleigh! Jin - gle bells Oh Jin - gle bells Oh Jin - gle all the

Jin - gle bells! Jin - gle bells! Jin- gle bells! one - horse o - pen
way! Oh what fun it is to ride in a one - horse o - pen
way! Oh what fun what fun it is to ride in a one - horse o - pen
f
>
f
sleigh! Jin - gle bells Oh Jing! (ng) Jin - gle bells Oh
sleigh!
>
pp
mf
Jing! (ng) Jin - gle Jin - gle Jin - gle Jin - gle Jin - gle bells Oh
p
gradually crescendo to the fortissimo
Jin - gle bells Oh Jin - gle bells Oh Jin - gle bells Oh Jin-gle all the
way! Oh what fun it is to ride in a one - horse o - pen

sleigh!
Jin - gle bells Oh Jin - gle bells Oh Jin - gle all the

ff
one - horse o - pen
way! Oh what fun it is to ride in a
one - horse o - pen
one!
one - horse o - pen

Solo
Jin - gle Jin - gle
sleigh!
Jin - gle bells Oh Jing!
sleigh!
One-horse o - pen
Jin - gle bells Oh Jing!
One-horse o - pen sleigh!
Jin - gle bells Oh Jing!
sleigh!

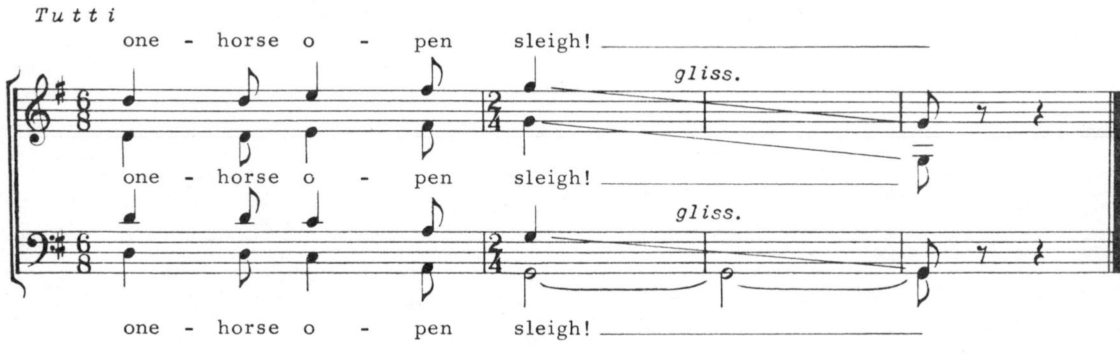
Tutti
one - horse o - pen sleigh!
gliss.
one - horse o - pen sleigh!
gliss.
one - horse o - pen sleigh!

Joy to the World

Isaac Watts, 1719

George F. Handel
Arranged by Lowell Mason

1. Joy to the world! the Lord is come;
   Let earth receive her King;
   Let ev'ry heart prepare Him room,
   And heav'n and nature sing.

2. Joy to the world! the Savior reigns;
   Let men their songs employ;
   While fields and floods, rocks, hills and plains,
   Repeat the sounding joy.

3. No more let sin and sorrow grow,
   Nor thorns infest the ground;
   He comes to make His blessings flow
   Far as the curse is found.

4. He rules the world with truth and grace,
   And makes the nations prove
   The glories of His righteousness,
   And wonders of His love.

Lovely Evening

Masters In This Hall

Old English Carol
Arranged by James McKelvy

For instruments*

*Available as octavo MF 852 for soprano and alto.

O Come All Ye Faithful

17th Century Latin Hymn
English by F. Oakley

18th Century hymn tune

O come, all ye faithful,
Joyful and triumphant,
O come ye, O come ye to Bethlehem.
Come and behold Him,
Born the King of Angels:
O come let us adore Him,
O come let us adore Him,
O come let us adore Him,
Christ the Lord.

Sing, choirs of angels,
Sing in exultation,
Sing all ye citizens of heav'n above:
Glory to God
In the highest, glory!
O come let us adore Him,
O come let us adore Him,
O come let us adore Him,
Christ the Lord.

Adeste fideles,
Laeti triumphantes;
Venite, venite in Bethlehem;
Natum videte,
Regem angelorum:
Venite adoremus,
Venite adoremus,
Venite adoremus
Dominum.

Cantet nunc Io!
Chorus angelorum;
Cantet nunc aula coelestium:
Gloria, Gloria
In excelsis Deo!
Venite adoremus,
Venite adoremus,
Venite adoremus
Dominum.

O Come, O Come Immanuel

12th Century French
English by John Neale

8th Century Gregorian

1. O come, O come, Immanuel,
And ransom captive Israel,
That mourns in lonely exile here
Until the Son of God appear.
Rejoice! Rejoice! Immanuel
Shall come to thee, O Israel.

2. O come, Thou Rod of Jesse, free
Thine own from Satan's tyranny;
From depths of hell thy people save,
And give them vic't'ry o'er the grave.
Rejoice.....

3. O come, Thou Day-Spring, come and cheer
Our spirits by Thine advent here;
Disperse the gloomy clouds of night,
And death's dark shadows put to flight.
Rejoice.....

4. O come, O come, Thou Lord of might,
Who to Thy tribes, on Sinai's height,
In ancient times did'st give the Law,
In cloud, and majesty and awe.
Rejoice.....

O Little Town of Bethlehem

Phillips Brooks, 1868

Lewis H. Redner, 1868

O little town of Bethlehem,
How still we see thee lie!
Above thy deep and dreamless sleep
The silent stars go by;
Yet is thy dark street shineth
The everlasting Light;
The hopes and fears of all the years
Are met in thee tonight.

O holy Child of Bethlehem,
Descend to us, we pray;
Cast out our sin and enter in,
Be born in us today.
We hear the Christmas angels
The great glad tidings tell:
Oh, come to us, abide with us,
Our Lord Emmanuel!

O Sanctissima

J. Falk, 1810

Sicilian Hymn

Oh, how joyfully, Oh, how merrily
Christmas comes with its grace divine!
Grace again is beaming, Christ the world redeeming:
Hail, ye Christians, hail the joyous Christmastime!

O Tannenbaum

Traditional German Carol

1. O Tannenbaum, O Tannenbaum,
   Wie treu sind deine Blätter!
   Du grünst nicht nur zur Sommerzeit,
   Nein, auch im Winter, wenn es schneit.
   O Tannenbaum, O Tannenbaum,
   Wie treu sind deine Blätter!

2. O Tannenbaum, O Tannenbaum,
   Du kannst mir sehr gefallen!
   Wie oft hat mich zur Weihnachtszeit
   Ein Baum von dir mich hoch erfreut!
   O Tannenbaum, O Tannenbaum,
   Du kannst mir sehr gefallen!

3. O Tannenbaum, O Tannenbaum,
   Dein Kleid soll mich was lehren!
   Die Hoffnung und Beständigkeit
   Gibt Trost und Kraft zu aller Zeit.
   O Tannenbaum, O Tannenbaum,
   Sein Kleid soll mich was lehren!

Silent Night

Joseph Möhr, 1818 — Franz Gruber

1. Stille Nacht, Heilige nacht!
   Alles schläft, einsam wacht
   Nur das traute hochheilige Paar.
   Holder Knabe im lockigen Haar,
   Schlaf in himmlischer Ruh,
   Schlaf in himmlischer Ruh!

2. Stille Nacht, heilige Nacht!
   Hirten erst kundgemacht!
   Durch der Engel Halleluja
   Tönt es laut vonffern und nah:
   Christ, der Retter, ist da,
   Christ, der Retter, is da!

3. Stille Nacht, heilige Nacht!
   Gottes Sohn, O, wie lacht
   Lieb aus deinem göttlichen Mund,
   Da uns schlägt die rettende Stund,
   Christ, in deiner Geburt,
   Christ, in deiner Geburt.

1. Silent night, Holy night!
   All is calm, all is bright
   Round yon virgin Mother and Child
   Holy Infant so tender and mild,
   Sleep in heavenly peace,
   Sleep in heavenly peace!

2. Silent night, holy night,
   Shepherds quake at the sight;
   Glories stream from heaven a far,
   Heavenly hosts sing alleluia,
   Christ the Savior, is born!
   Christ, the Savior, is born!

3. Silent night, holy night,
   Son of God, love's pure light
   Radiant beams from Thy holy face,
   With the dawn of redeeming grace,
   Jesus, Lord, at Thy birth,
   Jesus, Lord, at Thy birth.

We Three Kings

John H. Hopkins Jr., 1857

KINGS:

1. We three kings of Orient are,
   Bearing gifts we traverse far
   Field and fountain, moor and mountain,
   Following yonder star.

Refrain: Oh, star of wonder, star of might,
Star with royal beauty bright,
Westward leading, still proceeding,
Guide us to the perfect light.

MELCHIOR:

2. Born a babe on Bethlehem's plain,
   Gold we bring to crown Him again;
   King forever, ceasing never,
   Over us all to reign.

CASPER:

3. Frankincense to offer have I;
   Incense owns a Deity nigh,
   Pray'r and praising all men raising,
   Worship God on high.

BALTHAZAR:

4. Myrrh is mine; its bitter perfume
   Breathes a life of gath'ring gloom;
   Sorrowing, sighing, bleeding, dying,
   Sealed in the stonecold tomb.

ALL:

5. Glorious now behold Him rise,
   King and God and Sacrifice;
   Heav'n sings "Hallelujah!"
   "Hallelujah!" earth replies.

We Wish You a Merry Christmas

7/8 METER The eighth note must remain equal in time value whether it is in a group of two (♪♪) or three (♪♪♪). The resulting irregular accents create a very lilting rhythm. It is suggested that the 7-8 section be learned with a metronome set at about 152, gradually increasing the tempo to about 208. The signs L and Δ indicate two and three note accent groups.

Traditional Text

Music arranged by James McKelvy

What Child is This?

William C. Dix

Old English Air
Arranged by John Stainer

1. What Child is this, Who, laid to rest
   On Mary's lap is sleeping?
   Whom angels greet with anthems sweet,
   While shepherds watch are keeping?

Refrain: This, this is Christ the King;
Whome shepherds guard and angels sing:
Haste, haste to bring Him laud,
The Babe, the Son of Mary!

2. Why lies He in such mean estate,
   Where ox and ass are feeding?
   Good Christian, fear: for sinners here
   The silent Word is pleading:

3. So bring Him incense, gold, myrrh,
   Come peasant, king to own Him;
   The King of kings salvation brings;
   Let loving hearts enthrone Him.

While Shepherds Watched Their Flocks

Nahum Tate, 1700

Based on music by
George Friedrich Handel

1. While shepherds watch'd their flocks by night,
   All seated on the ground,
   The angel of the Lord came down,
   And glory shone around.

2. "Fear not!" said he; for mighty dread
   Had seized their troubled mind,
   Glad tidings of great joy I bring,
   To you and all mankind.

3. "To you, in David's town, this day
   Is born of David's line,
   The Savior who is Christ the Lord;
   And this shall be the sign.

4. "The heav'nly Babe you there shall find
   To human view display'd,
   All meanly wrapp'd in swathing bands,
   And in a manger laid."

INDEX

Titles in CAPITAL LETTERS
First lines in lower case letters